JE
PROTOPOPESC
PERILOUS PIT

14.00   1993

W9-BGI-265

THE PERILOUS PIT

THE PERILOUS PIT

By Orel Odinov Protopopescu

Illustrated by Jacqueline Chwast

GREEN TIGER PRESS
Published by Simon & Schuster
New York London Toronto Sydney Tokyo Singapore

GREEN TIGER PRESS
Simon & Schuster Building, Rockefeller Center
1230 Avenue of the Americas, New York, New York 10020
Text copyright © 1993 by Orel Odinov Protopopescu
Illustrations copyright © 1993 by Jacqueline Chwast
All rights reserved including the right of reproduction
in whole or in part in any form.
GREEN TIGER PRESS is an imprint of Simon & Schuster.
Designed by Alan Benjamin
Manufactured in the United States of America

10 9 8 7 6 5 4 3 2 1

Library of Congress Cataloging-in-Publication Data
Protopopescu, Orel Odinov. The perilous pit / by Orel Protopopescu;
illustrated by Jacqueline Chawst.   p.   cm.   Summary: When Katie tosses
a peach pit over her shoulder, it sets off a series of ridiculous events.
[1. Humorous stories.] I. Chwast, Jacqueline, ill. II. Title.   PZ7.P9438Pe
1993 [E]—dc20 92-290 CIP ISBN: 0-671-76910-3

336733

To Josephine "Joi" Nobisso,
friend and colleague,
who cleared the way for me
on this far from perilous path.
O.O.P.

For my brother, Stanley
J.C.

One hot June day,
Katie sat under a tree
reading a book
and eating a peach,
and when she got down
to the last sweet bite,

she threw away the pit—
not straight ahead,
not to her right,
nor to her left
where the story
might have stopped,
but over her shoulder,
not watching where it went,
and that's how it became

the perilous pit—
for the pit hit a cat
who ran into the street
and made a car bump
into a fireplug
that spouted like a whale
all over the street
where daredevil Danny
was riding his skateboard,

and he rode that wave
down a big hill
and into the yard
where Mrs. Lavar
was hanging up her wash,

and, wrapped in a sheet,
Danny went his way
straight past the theater
where **Haunted** was playing

UNTED

and the people coming out
were so stunned
by Danny in his sheet
they gasped and screamed
and fainted in a heap,

and their popcorn flew up
like a swarm of bees
as a sudden gust
filled Danny's sheet
and, as ambulances whined
and firetrucks clanged,

Danny and that popcorn
sailed across the bay
and out into the sea
where whales spouted free
as broken fireplugs,
and the birds drawn
by his popcorn trail
danced through the spray

POPC

and were spotted by a pilot
flying through the clouds,
and when he saw the boy
skimming the surf
he called the Navy

who called the Coast Guard

who called the Air Force

and, as planes zoomed
and ships blew their horns,
a helicopter dropped
a ladder to the boy
who climbed through a cloud
until he was safe
and flying over the sea
and over the bay
and over the town
of streets washed clean
of everything but

people telling stories
of crazy cats
and tidal waves
and ghosts on wheels
and boys with wings,

and he flew over Mrs. Lavar
who was taking down her wash,
and over the firefighters
turning off the fireplug,

and just before he landed
on the village green,
he flew over the tree
where little Katie sat
reading her book,
peaceful as you please,
and eating a peach,
a peachy ripe peach,
right down to the pit.

HAUNTED

And then . . .

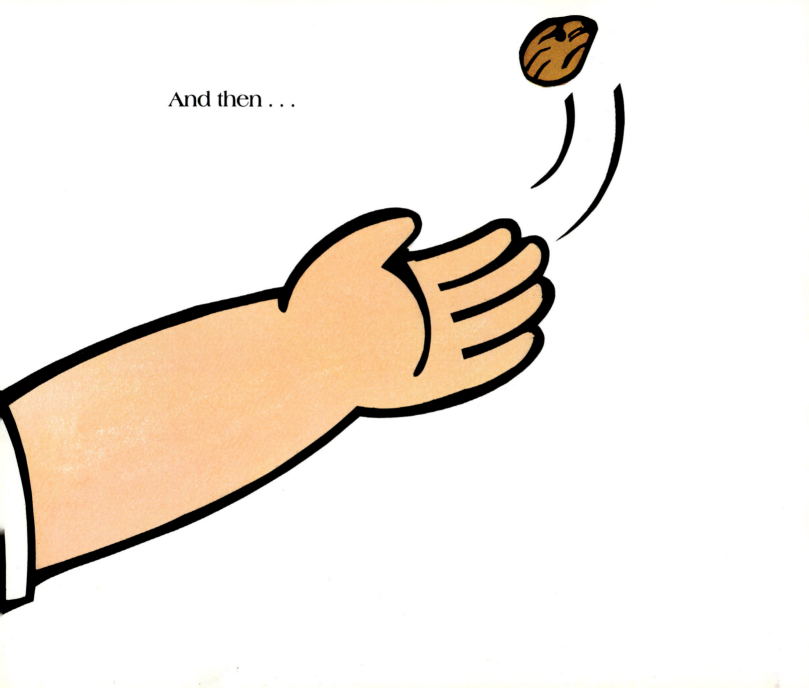